WHAT WOULD YOU DO?

WHAT DID Carey DO?

Rachel,
Have fun sharing this tale w/ your family
and friends!

6·26·19

By Jeffery R. Kellam

Jeffery Kellam

Illustrated by

Madison F. Nevil

WHAT WOULD You DO?
WHAT DID Carey DO?

ISBN: 9781095888407

ACKNOWLEDGEMENTS: This book would not have been possible without the inspiring story from my dear friend Carey Ewanik, the help and encouragement of my wife Carolyn, the support of my best friend and prayer-partner Mark Nevil, the gifted interpretative artwork of very funny and witty super-skilled and creative Illustrator Madison (Maddy) Nevil, and Graphic Artist Gage Ballard with the support of Graphic Arts Instructor Mr. David Brace and Principal Mr. Jon Higgins of the High School Heartland Career Center Wabash, Indiana, USA.

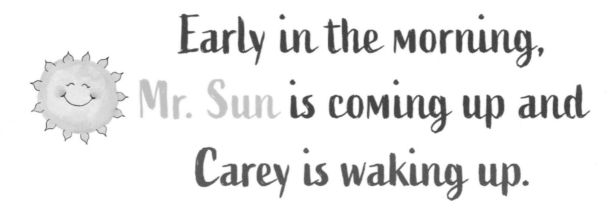

Early in the morning,
Mr. Sun is coming up and
Carey is waking up.

Do YOU wake up early
in the morning when Mr. Sun
is coming up?

Carey wanted to have fun, so he decided to go fishing.

Would **YOU** have fun going fishing?

Notice that Carey left clothes out on the floor when he was getting ready.

Do **YOU** leave clothes out on the floor when **YOU** are getting ready?

Carey reached the stream and he didn't have any rubber hip-waders.

Carey had to wade in the stream to fish, but he didn't want to get his pants wet.

What would You do if You needed to wade in the stream but You didn't have any rubber hip-waders?

What did Carey do?

Carey decided to take his pants off so they wouldn't get wet before he waded in the stream.

Would **You** take **Your** pants off so they wouldn't get wet before **You** waded in the stream?

Carey was excited! He caught his first Mr. Fishy! 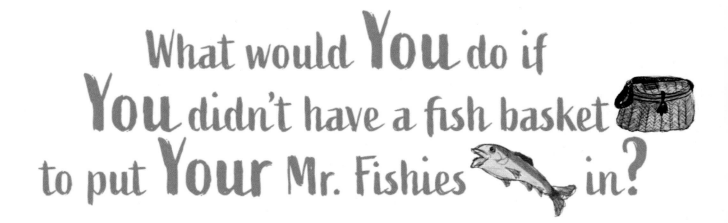 Would You be excited if You caught Your first Mr. Fishy?

But Carey didn't have a fish basket to put his Mr. Fishies in.

What would You do if You didn't have a fish basket to put Your Mr. Fishies in?

What did Carey do?

Since Carey didn't have a fish basket, he hung Mr. Fishy on a branch.

If **You** didn't have a fish basket, would **You** hang Mr. Fishy on a branch?

Carey was excited! He continued to catch Mr. Fishies!

Would **You** be excited if **You** continued to catch Mr. Fishies?

Carey continued
to hang his Mr. Fishies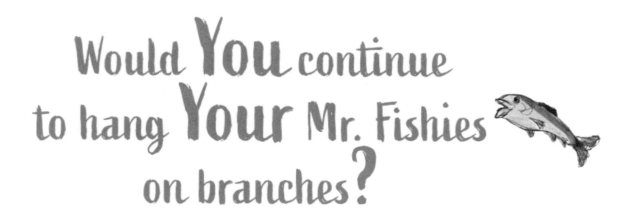
on branches.

Would YOU continue
to hang YOUR Mr. Fishies
on branches?

Carey had to take his Mr. Fishies home, but he didn't have a fish basket to carry them in.

What would You do if You had to take Your Mr. Fishies home and You didn't have a fish basket to carry them in?

What did Carey do?

Carey tied knots in his pants' legs, put his Mr. Fishies into each pant leg, and swung his pants over his shoulder to carry his Mr. Fishies home.

Would **You** tie knots in **Your** pants' legs to carry **Your** Mr. Fishies home?

When Carey returned home, he
showed his Mr. Fishies
to his Mom and asked her to
cook them for supper.

When You returned home, would You
show Your Mr. Fishies
to Your Mom and ask her to
cook them for supper?

That evening Carey and his Mom
and Dad had Mr. Fishies
for supper. Yum yum!

Would **You** have Mr. Fishies
for supper with **Your** Mom and Dad?

Would those Mr. Fishies be yummy?

After a fun-filled
day when Mr. Sun
was going down, Carey went
to bed and fell asleep.

After a fun-filled
day when Mr. Sun
is going down, will You go
to bed and fall asleep?

ABOUT THE AUTHOR: Jeffery Kellam grew up nearby the Salamonie Reservoir in rural Wabash County, Indiana, USA. In the summers, Jeff and his childhood friends liked to go camping, fishing, and hunting. Jeff's favorite adult sport for several decades has been Morel mushroom hunting with ice fishing being a close 2nd. Jeff has been Blessed with his wonderful wife Carolyn and wonderful children and grandchildren.

STORYLINE INSPIRATION: The inspiration for this whimsical true story came from Jeff's dear friend, Carey Ewanik. Carey grew up in and presently resides nearby Edmonton, Alberta, Canada. One day Jeff asked Carey if he fished and hunted when he was younger. Carey responded, "Did I ever!" and went on to tell Jeff this story. Jeff was so fascinated with this true tale he immediately began to share it with others. This resulted with all the listeners regardless of their ages becoming tickled. Jeff then decided to set this story in writing as a special gift to his friend Carey. As Jeff proceeded, he then saw the need to write this children's book to share this very hilarious story that shows imaginative and creative ways to solve problems. Whether you are young or old, Jeff hopes You have the same feelings of overjoy and elation when You read and share this true telltale with Your children, family, and friends.

ABOUT THE ILLUSTRATOR: Madison Nevil was reared in rural Wabash County, Indiana, USA. Madison has been interested in drawing ever since her early childhood. Madison currently is a student at Ball State University's School of Art, Muncie, Indiana, USA. Madison enjoys creating still-life art, and animal-related drawings.

ABOUT THE GRAPHIC ARTIST: Gage Ballard was born in Lafayette, Indiana, USA and has lived in several places throughout Indiana, USA. Gage has always leaned towards the artistic side of life and graduates May 2019 from Wabash High School and Heartland Career Center Graphic Arts Design, Wabash, Indiana, USA. Gage will attend Purdue University Game Development and Design, Lafayette, Indiana, USA. Gage appreciates that his life's journey has led to his Calling of inspiring others with his art, which he hopes to do throughout his lifetime.

58736958R00018

Made in the USA
Columbia, SC
23 May 2019